Lessons Learned In Jumbo Valley

SHERRY WYNE

Lessons Learned In Jumbo Valley

Copyright © 2018 Sherry Wyne

All rights reserved.

Scripture quotations from The Authorized (King James) Version. Rights in the Authorized Version in the United Kingdom are vested in the Crown. Reproduced by permission of the Crown's patentee, Cambridge University Press.

No part of this publication may be reproduced, distributed, or transmitted in any form or by any means, including photocopying, recording, or other electronic or mechanical methods, without the prior written permission of the author/publisher, except in the case of brief quotations embodied in critical reviews and certain other noncommercial uses permitted by copyright law.

DEDICATION

To my Parents, Sisters and Brother
Along with each extended Family member
Who has loved and supported me all these years.

I Love You All!

TABLE OF CONTENTS

INTRODUCTION 7

1 LESSONS LEARNED 9

2 VALLEY GIRL 16

3 IT JUST COMES NATURALLY 26

4 LOOKS CAN BE DECEIVING 32

5 THE POWER OF PERCEPTION 37

6 WHERE POWER RESIDES 41

7 GOD OF THE VALLEY 46

8 TEST OR TRIAL 50

9 GRAVITY OR PRESSURE 51

10 THE PRINCIPLE THING 55

11 ONE MOUNTAIN AT A TIME 59

12 THE PURPOSE OF A SHADOW 62

13 UP EXALTED MOUNTAINS 67

THE RED SEA EXPERIENCE 73

14 THE RED SEA VS THE JORDAN 75

15 PRESSURIZED SAINTS 80

16 ACROSS IMPASSIBLE RIVERS 84

17 THE CONCLUSION OF THE MATTER 88

18 A TUMBLE FROM THE TOP 90

LESSONS LEARNED AS A CHILD 98

ABOUT THE AUTHOR 101

INTRODUCTION

Memories are funny things. They can take you to places you never wanted to go again and leave you feeling angry and depressed. Sometimes they bring a touch of sadness mixed with happiness at the fleeting remembrance of a departed loved one. Or they can bring a smile to your face when a humorous memory pops unexpectedly into your mind. And on occasion they can encapsulate a moment in time, like a snow-globe, and allow you to look back on that moment from a different perspective. That is what happened to me one evening in Bible Class when our Pastor asked if anyone could remember God speaking to them or calling them into ministry when they were children. Several people stood to share their childhood memories.

While they were talking a picture of me as a young girl flashed through my mind. I was crouched down on a rock in the river that flowed beside my childhood home in West Virginia. Trees shadowed the river's banks but in the middle where I was playing the sun was shining down bathing me in its golden light. In that forgotten, flashback moment I literally saw the presence of God hovering over me! What a surprise to realize that He had been with me all along.

That picture has invaded my mind many times since then and every time it does I feel a sense of awe. Why would God spend so much time with a young child whose greatest joy was to run wild up and down mountains and back and forth across rivers? Because He knew that someday I would need help climbing a spiritual mountain or crossing a spiritual river. And so, God took the time to teach me natural lessons from the elements around me. Years later, He revealed the spiritual meanings of those lessons and commissioned me to write, *Lessons Learned in Jumbo Valley.*

And being the obedient child of God that I am, or that I try to be, I wrote the book. For several years it "rested" in a desk drawer. Then one Memorial Weekend I had an accident while trying to take a picture of a waterfall and took a twenty-five foot swan-dive through the air without the aid of a parachute! God caught me in His hands, healed my broken bones and taught me a few more lessons. That's when I realized that it was time for the book to come out of hiding!

1 LESSONS LEARNED

<u>Lesson</u>: "An instance or experience from which useful knowledge may be gained."

(Funk & Wagnall's Standard Desk Dictionary)

God is in the lesson-giving business! He gives us these lessons so that spiritual knowledge can be gained for the purposes of instruction and for empowerment in a time of personal testing, to strengthen natural or spiritual family members and more often than not, to aid and comfort total strangers. There are times when we have to learn a lesson the hard way and then there are times when we're having so much fun that we don't even realize that a lesson is being taught. Thankfully, I had fun learning!

Think of the wise proverbs of Solomon and the sowing parables of Jesus. They use natural teachings to emphasize spiritual points. While I was playing, God was teaching me natural lessons that He would one day reveal as spiritual laws. Now, I'm not comparing myself to Solomon or Jesus, BUT I do believe God has given me some principles that will be a blessing to you.

One of the greatest lessons I have learned is how perception affects the outcome of our spiritual tests and trials. Our perception will cause us to have either a positive outlook or a negative one. A negative outlook will bring defeat in our spiritual valley, guarantee failure on the way up our spiritual mountain and deny us access to the other side of our spiritual river.

On the other hand, a positive outlook will enable us to see the valley as a place of power and to view our spiritual mountains and rivers with anticipation instead of fear. It's all in how you look at it because - what you see is what you get!

I've learned that there is only one way to get somewhere in a spiritual promise land. That is by going up and down, up and down and up and down again. A great man, Dr. Martin Luther King Jr., once said, "I have been to the mountaintop..." The fact that he used "have been" meant that he was no longer on the mountaintop. He knew there were other mountains to conquer, and in order to do that he had to come down and start again.

We hate starting over again don't we? But in order to get from one end of a mountain range to the other end, we must go up and down and start and stop, constantly. That is the *only* way to travel in a land of mountains and valleys and our spiritual promise land just happens to be full of both. So, the only way to make progress is by going from the valley to the mountaintop, to the valley, to the mountaintop, to the valley...!

Can you climb two mountains at the same time? Neither can I! God taught me that we can only accomplish in the spiritual realm what has been done, or what can be done in the natural realm. This is a Divine principle and will be discussed in great detail later in the book. What it means is no matter how many mountains or tests there are, you only have to climb the one God has ordained for that time.

I loved playing in the river that ran by our house even more than I loved climbing mountains and it is from that river that I learned the greatest spiritual lesson of my life. The sound of the water running down the riverbed was a consistent, day in – day out presence in my life. At times it was a soft tinkling putting me to sleep at night. Other times it was bubbling, as if overflowing with laughter and joy. After the winter snows melted, the water rose and its music became louder, insistent on being heard. But there was always the *sound*.

Revelation 1:15, *"And his voice as the sound of many waters."*

Isaiah 66:6 *"A voice of noise from the city, a voice from the temple, a voice of the LORD that rendereth recompense to his enemies."*

There are many voices competing for our attention and at times it is hard to distinguish one from another. From my beloved river I learned how to recognize the voice of God from among the mix. What greater lesson could God have taught a child? As far as I am concerned, there isn't one. My life depends on my ability to hear the voice of God. Spiritual application of natural lessons would not have been learned and this book would not have been written if I had not heard the voice of God.

Stepping from one rock to another up and down the river was one of my favorite pastimes. The challenge was not to fall in, but often I would step on a rock that was slick and down I would go. Other times, I had to retrace my steps because I had boxed myself in. From that game, God taught me about the need for a sure foundation and how to plan beyond my next step. Judging from some of my past failures you would not think that I was very good at choosing the best paths to travel but while I was playing in the river, I was very good at it.

God taught me as a child how to climb mountains and get across rivers. However, down through the years I developed two major phobias. I am scared to death of high places and I panic when I get in water up to my kneecaps! In other words, the fun things God used to teach me life lessons while I was growing up are the very things Satan has made me most fearful of as an adult. He knows that if I am afraid of them in the natural realm, I will be afraid of them in the spiritual realm as well.

The next time you find yourself fearful of something, whether it's public speaking, climbing a high mountain, leading a praise service, stepping out into a deep river or any other situation that makes you afraid, stop and think. Could it be that the devil has tricked you so that you won't use your God-given gift? I'm just going to go ahead right now and say, "Amen" for you!

Did you know that you could know something for years and years and not know that you know it? God taught me these lessons before I was ten years old, but it wasn't until many years later that He gave me the revelation of their spiritual meaning. After being saved for six years a test came my way that almost destroyed me. It was during that time that God showed me why He had taught me those specific lessons and how I could apply them to overcome the test.

It began one day while I was flicking the channels on TV and came across an Elvis Presley special. His music always made me feel happy and on that day I was in dire need of some happiness. He was singing, "This Time You Gave Me a Mountain". The chorus goes like this…

"This time, Lord, you gave me a mountain,
A mountain that I may never climb.
It isn't a hill any longer,
You gave me a mountain this time."

That song summed up my situation perfectly. I was facing a mountain whose top seemed to reach the heavens and there didn't appear to be any way over it. A few days later at work that song started running through my mind, over and over again. By that time, I wasn't speaking to God and I didn't think He was speaking to me! I was angry with Him because I felt He had allowed the situation to happen. So when the devil started hammering my mind with the words of that song, I believed him. I had no hope of climbing that mountain, much less of reaching its top.

Then Satan laughed and said, "It looks like He did give

you a mountain this time, doesn't it?" My mouth actually dropped open. What Nerve! The devil was blaming God for the situation that he had arranged in my life. It never occurred to me that I was doing the same thing! But at the time, I was so overcome with disappointment and anger that I couldn't defend God or myself. I was speechless.

But the Holy Spirit wasn't!

Immediately, the God in me spoke back to Satan and said, "Devil, you forgot. I grew up climbing mountains." He left rather quickly!

I was stunned, not only by the fact that God had answered for me but also by the revelation of what He was saying. God had reminded the devil that I was used to climbing natural mountains which meant that I was capable of climbing spiritual ones also. Encouraged by what God had said to the devil, I decided to get a little mouthy myself. I said, "Yeah, devil, you forgot, I grew up climbing mountains."

The Lord spoke back to me and said, "No, Sherry, he didn't forget. You did. It was a mistake on Satan's part to remind you of what you were taught, but you are the one who forgot. I taught you how to climb mountains and get over rivers before you were ten years old. You have no excuse!"

That conversation with God resulted in this book. He taught me everything I needed to know about climbing mountains and crossing rivers but somewhere between childhood and adulthood I had forgotten the lessons.

I thought about the walnut. In order to get the meat of

the nut out you have to break the shell around it. The situation in my life broke me but in the process, knowledge that had been planted long ago escaped the imprisonment of my mind. Then from a spiritual standpoint, I began to re-learn the natural lessons God taught me as a child. And what a child I was!

2 VALLEY GIRL

When you go to a doctor for a medical condition you want to know about that doctor's credentials. When you need a lawyer you want one who graduated with honors from law school. When you go to a minister for spiritual guidance you want to know that he is in touch with God. And when you have someone telling you that they can teach you how to climb spiritual mountains and cross spiritual rivers, you want to know what kind of experiences they have had. I offer this resume.

West Virginia, the "Mountain State", is the only state in America that lies entirely within the Appalachian Mountain range. It has the highest average elevation of any state east of the Mississippi and boasts of an endless supply of mountains, rivers and valleys. West Virginia is famous for its scenic beauty, coal mines, logging industry and its poverty. During the early 1960s, it was one of the poorest states nationwide. It was there in a small town called Webster Springs that my twin sister, Nancy and I were born.

If you are born in West Virginia, you are a "hillbilly". That probably conjures up images of Jed Clampet, Granny, and the other members of the TV show, The Beverly

Hillbillies. Some of those images are true - most are not. Of all the cultures in the world, hillbillies are probably looked down on more than any other. Stereotyped as toothless, stupid, dirty and lazy snuff-chewers, hillbillies are also said to have uneven legs from all of their mountain climbing. To the contrary, I have a mouth full of teeth, I am intelligent, I take baths regularly, hold a full-time job and have never chewed snuff in my life. But I do have to confess, I think one of my legs is longer than the other one!

My parents never married and some might say that my twin and I were an accident. I have never wasted one day in my life feeling bad about that! I believe that everything happens for a reason and that God planned my entrance into this world. Only He knows where destiny will take me and only He knows what and whom it will take to get me there.

My sister and I were identical twins. An Aunt told me that they had to keep bracelets on us to tell us apart. Unfortunately, my sister developed pneumonia when she was four months old and died. The day they buried her, my father left West Virginia and never returned. I can't imagine the pain that must have caused my mother, to lose her child and the man she loved at the same time. But she went on and for that and many other reasons I have always admired her. I met my biological father again when I was twenty-two years old. I was grateful that God had used him to give me life but there was no bond between us and we didn't keep in touch. In September of 1994, my Father, homeless and alone, died from coronary disease brought on by alcoholism. When I think about where I would be if he had married my Mother, I have to stop and thank God for those He put in my life and for those He took out.

Mom and I lived with her mother until 1957 when she married my stepfather. From their union I was blessed with two sisters and a brother and God didn't give me just anybody, He gave me the absolute best! When they were first married, we lived in a tiny house at the top of Hodum Mountain, which towered above neighboring mountains at over 2,500 feet. The curvy road by our house was well traveled since it was the main route to Buchannon, one of the largest cities near us. When I was about three years old I decided to visit my Granny who lived on Lick Run. Somehow I slipped away without Mom seeing me and headed down Hodum Mountain. A semi-truck driver stopped and asked my Mother if she had lost a little girl because he had seen one going down the road. I received a good whipping for that but it didn't curb my enthusiasm for exploration!

We moved near my stepfather's parents in Jumbo in the fall of 1957. My grandparent's home was nestled between two mountains in a narrow valley that had a river running through it. At one time a logging camp had existed there but all that was left was a large pile of sawdust. Mom and Dad built a small house across the river from Granny and Pappy. It had two bedrooms, a kitchen and a living room and was heated by a pot-bellied stove. The bathroom was outside next to the pigpen!

During that time Dad was offered a job in a steel mill in

Ohio. Twice a month for several years he traveled back and forth from Ohio to West Virginia to be with us. Our Grandparents had relocated so Mom and the four of us moved into their old house. It had three bedrooms, a dining room, a kitchen and a living room. Again there was the pot-bellied stove and the outhouse. There was a small country store about a mile down the road and a tiny Pentecostal Church up the river from us. We could hear the congregation singing and shouting from our front porch. We had chickens, horses and pigs to care for along with our dog, Rover, and a couple of pet goats. I had a bike to ride, mountains to climb and a river to play in. It was a great place to be a kid!

It was in that place that God taught me how to climb mountains and cross rivers. As I said earlier, we lived in a house at the foot of a mountain. Therefore, I lived in a Valley. Our house was fenced in on one side by Hodum Mountain and separated from the unnamed mountain on the opposite side by a river. To the front and back, mountains loomed in the distance. So the first thing you saw when you walked outside, whether you went out the front door or the side door was a mountain. Automatically, you would look up and I really believe that all of those years of looking up have helped to develop my optimistic outlook!

To me that little valley was one of the most beautiful places on earth. The brilliant blue sky and the vibrant greens of tree-covered mountains would make any artist take brush in hand. Butterflies and birds of various species added their colors to those of the rose and honeysuckle bushes that grew around our yard. At night the sky was like a planetarium and the singing of the crickets along with the gurgling of the river lulled us to sleep. It was indeed a place of beauty and tranquility.

Thank God and Dad the old homestead is still standing! I go back to visit at least twice a year. Here is something you might not know about hillbillies, very few of them can stay away from their birthplace for long periods of time. The land seems to call our names and we have to go *home*. Over the years few things have changed. Of course, the animals are gone, along with the fences that kept them contained. Some of the outside buildings have been torn down and others put up. The sawdust pile that we loved to play in as children has been leveled and a new cement bridge connects us to the neighbors across the river. An oil furnace has replaced the pot-bellied stove and another room has been added off of the dining room. Flicking the wall switch now turns on the lights as opposed to pulling a string that's tied between the socket and the bed rail. There is only one of those left and if I have anything to say about it, it will stay that way! And finally, a corner of the porch has been enclosed and turned into a small bathroom. However, there is still an outhouse for those brave enough to use it. With all the time that has gone past and all the changes that have been made, that little valley remains still - the most beautiful place on earth!

As a child I had no fear. The mountains and river were my playground and I would run from one adventure to another. But looking back now, I realize my wanderlust must have caused my mom a lot of stress. She was raising the four of us, myself, Florence (Punk), Floyd (Bud) and Kathy (Sissy) alone since Dad was living and working in Ohio. He was saving money to buy a house there and I appreciate the sacrifices he made to create a better life for us but that left Mom with her hands full.

Mom didn't drive at the time and the nearest town with a hospital, Webster Springs, was twelve miles away. So when Bud threw a rock and cut Sissy's head open, Mom was the doctor. When Punk was fishing and somehow managed to run a hook all the way through her thumb, Mom took a chisel and a hammer and cut off the end of the hook and pulled it out. I can almost hear my sister screaming now! When I caught my hand in the wringer washer and almost tore my thumb off, it was Mom who carried me up the road to the neighbors to get a ride to the hospital. After those and many other instances, you would think that my mother would be afraid to let us leave her side. But she never stopped us from exploring the exciting world around us, and for that she has my undying love and gratitude!

My sisters and brother and I loved playing on the sawdust pile next to our house. In the summer, the sawdust would get so hot that you could hardly walk across it. We would climb to the top, hopping and skipping to keep our feet from burning and jump down into it's soft, warm bottom. When we finished playing we were covered with sawdust. It was all through our hair and even in our underwear. We weren't the only ones that liked the sawdust pile though. Copperheads and other snakes liked to sun themselves there so Mom made us stop playing in it. Naturally, being kids we would sneak and go to that forbidden place. Thank God for angels!

With all of the rivers in West Virginia, bridges are a big part of any hillbilly's life. My siblings and I spent a lot of happy times on the bridge between our former house and the new one. To us it was a fishing spot, a diving board and a perch from which to watch the hypnotic wanderings of Holly River. Over the years that bridge and a few others have been washed out by floods and replaced with newer wooden structures. A few years ago our neighbors decided to put in a cement bridge further down the river so they wouldn't have to drive through our yard to get to their house. When they told us I felt like someone had punched me in the stomach! A bridge had been in that spot for as long as I could remember and I couldn't imagine not having one there. Now mind you, I'm only there once or twice a year and it really shouldn't have mattered what I thought but out of the kindness of their hearts, the neighbors agreed to put the new bridge in the same place. They even wrote my initials in the cement!

Jumbo Bridge, another beloved spot, crossed Holly River just beyond our house. Before the trees in our yard grew so tall we could see the bridge and the church that was across the river from our porch. Near the bridge is a narrow, dirt road that leads up a mountain to Desert Forks, a once prosperous logging region. About half a mile up Desert Forks Road some of the mountain had been cleared off in a curve near the roadway to keep brush and trees from scratching passing cars. That small clearing became "our mountain"

The four of us had climbed most of the mountains around our home but this one was special. We would stand back as far as we could on the road, careful not to fall over the steep edge, take a running leap and try to make it up that little hill. It was only four or five feet high but we really felt like we had accomplished something when we reached the top. "Our mountain" was often muddy and there wasn't much to grab on to for support if you started sliding back down. That made it a little more challenging to climb. Or maybe it was because we were so young, my baby sister was five, my brother six, my other sister was eight and I was ten and we were all short and skinny! So climbing a five-foot mountain was quite a feat to us. When we go back home and walk up that dirt road, we still say, "There's our mountain"

My sisters and brother often went with me but for the most part, I explored alone. The river by our house was not very deep, except when it was flooded but it was fairly wide. I prided myself on being able to travel a good distance up and down it by stepping from rock to rock without falling in. That took a lot of skill. You couldn't just jump to any rock. Some were too small to hold my weight even though I was very tiny at the time. Others were slick with mud, which meant I would fall as soon as my foot hit the rock so I had to plan ahead. If I jumped to the rock on my left I had to make sure there was another one to jump to from there. I absolutely loved playing in that river and spent many happy hours there. Ironically, the only thing I didn't learn while playing in the river was how to swim!

As you can probably tell, I loved my valley home. The fact that it was buried between mountains and nearly surrounded by water never caused me a moment of fear. I was safe and happy there. Mountaintops beckoned, daring me to conquer their dizzying heights and I answered their summons. Holly River sang to my spirit of promised adventure and I followed the sound. I was a young child intent on one thing, having fun!

It didn't occur to me while I was having all this fun that God was teaching me principles for spiritual living. I failed to understand that I would have to learn to appreciate and love a spiritual valley as much as I did that little valley in Jumbo, West Virginia. I didn't stop to think that future spiritual mountains would be conquered only one way, by climbing them the same way I had climbed those around my childhood home. And not once did it enter my brain that the strategy I had used to cross Holly River would be the same strategy I would have to apply to my spiritual rivers.

In September of 1966, our family moved to a small town in Ohio. I was completely devastated to be pulled away from my beloved valley but God had a plan and destiny was calling. Decades later He unlocked the knowledge that had been stored in my childhood memories and taught me how to apply it in the spiritual realm.

Let me be your guide as we learn the principles that will

make travel in our spiritual promise land successful and maybe even a little enjoyable!

3 IT JUST COMES NATURALLY

Deuteronomy 11:11-12, *"But the land, whither ye go to possess it, is a land of hills and valleys, and drinketh water of the rain of heaven: A land which the Lord thy God careth for: the eyes of the Lord thy God are always upon it, from the beginning of the year unto the end of the year."*

The day we moved from West Virginia to Ohio ranks number one among the worst days of my young life. It broke my heart to leave but I was an eleven-year-old with no say in the matter. I blamed my stepfather for taking me away from my home and became very bitter towards him. From the day of that move until I was in my late twenties, we had a miserable relationship.

However, when I started learning more about God and His plan for my life, I discovered a startling truth. The Lord had used my stepfather to bring me to Ohio so that nine years later I would meet a man who would lead me to Christ. And though the relationship with the man didn't work out, the one with God did! In June of 1982, I was baptized in Jesus' Name and His precious blood washed away all of my sins. There is no feeling like being free of sin and guilt! Then God filled me with His Holy Spirit, and as my Pastor, Bishop Norman L. Wagner used to say, "The Holy Ghost is the *mind* or intellect of God." Afterward, I began to see the situation from a different perspective. If it hadn't been for my step dad bringing me to Ohio, I would not be where I am now, saved, blessed and doing what I love most, writing.

Still, at the time of the move I was devastated! I remember going out and sitting on the steps of our new house in Ohio. I looked around and all I could see was flat land. No mountains, no valleys, no rivers. I hated it! I felt like I was going to die.

When my Pastor prepares for a message he looks up key words in the dictionary and I've come to value that practice. So, throughout the book you will find definitions for very common words. I'm sure we all know the surface meaning of these words but some of the broader meanings really surprised me. And sometimes it was a connecting word in the different definitions that brought the concept of what God was saying together for me. Let's look at a few.

Valley: "An elongated depression on the earth's surface, usually between ranges of hills or mountains and often having a river or stream running along the bottom. An area drained by a river and its tributaries. A low point or condition." (Merriam Webster's Collegiate Dictionary)

River: "A large natural stream of water emptying into an ocean, a lake or another body of water and usually fed along its course by converging tributaries. A stream or abundant flow." (American Heritage Dictionary)

Mountain: "A natural elevation of the earth's surface having considerable mass, generally steep sides and a height greater than that of a hill. A large heap, a huge quantity." (American Heritage Dictionary)

The word "natural" appeared in the definition both for a mountain and a river. I knew it meant that rivers and mountains were from nature, or created by God. Therefore, it stood to reason that valleys were also natural. When I read the meaning for "natural" I began to see the big picture.

Natural: "Present in or produced by nature. Of, relating to, or concerning nature. Not acquired, inherent. Having a particular character by nature. (Biology) Expected and Accepted. (Noun) One having all the qualifications necessary for success. Suited by nature for a certain purpose or function." (American Heritage Dictionary)

The definition God spoke to my spirit about - *Expected and Accepted*!

The natural and the spiritual world work hand in hand. Did you ever stop to think that our Creator could have made us spirits with no physical or natural bodies? But He chose to breathe life into dirt and mankind became spiritual, natural creatures. We live and participate with God in the spiritual world but we exist in and are subject to in many ways, the natural world. Those worlds cannot be separated while we are on this earth.

In the natural world created by God, mountains, rivers and valleys are common components of the earth's surface. In the spiritual world, mountains, rivers and valleys represent spiritual tests and trials and low points in our Christian lives.

Mountains, rivers and valleys are natural and we know that God created them for a certain purpose or function. The same is true of their spiritual counterparts. God also creates them for a certain purpose and function. Since we know that natural mountains, rivers and valleys are "expected and accepted" as we travel this earth, then we know that their spiritual counterparts should be "expected and accepted" as we travel in that realm. The Bible says it like this,

1 Peter 4:12-13, *"Beloved, think it not strange concerning the fiery trial which is to try you, as though some strange thing happened to you: but rejoice,..."*.

However, our human instinct is not to "expect or accept" spiritual mountains, rivers or valleys. *If it isn't one thing, it's another. Here we go again! Every time I turn around, it's something else.* What do we really mean when we voice these common expressions? We're admitting that we are surprised each time there is a new test or trial in our lives. We are saying that we thought we would come to a point where there wouldn't be any more spiritual mountains, rivers or valleys. We believed that we could reach a level in God where we would not have to struggle, climb or get over Anything, Ever again!

But there are no flatlands in God, nor in the promise land He has given us!

Before God called Moses and the children of Israel out of Egypt, He prepared a promise land for them. The Bible points out that it was a land flowing with milk and honey, or a wealthy place. It was a land of hills and valleys and the water of the rain of heaven (rivers) nourished it. God was extremely proud of that land and bragged about how beautiful and fruitful it was. As a matter of fact, God thought this promise land to be the absolute best He had to offer. It was the place that would benefit them the most. And since all of the earth is the Lord's, He should know what He's talking about.

Therefore, since God thought that a land of mountains, rivers and valleys was the best He could give His children in a natural world, wouldn't He think that a land of mountains, rivers and valleys would be the best that He could give them in a spiritual world also? Absolutely! The next time you are complaining about tests and trials and you're screaming to get out of a valley, remember that God designed them for your benefit. Every spiritual mountain, river, and valley was tailor-made for you by a wise and loving God. And He's proud of it!

Let me re-emphasize; **Natural** means, "One having all of the qualifications necessary for success. One suited by nature (God) for a certain purpose or function." In other words, a natural being is one who has ALL it takes to succeed at whatever he or she was created to do.

The Biblical land of Canaan was full of hills, valleys and rivers, which meant there were natural conditions that the children of Israel had to conquer. But being natural creatures, they had all of the qualities necessary to overcome those obstacles. God knew they would have to climb mountains, cross rivers and struggle in valleys so He gave them natural bodies capable of such feats. You might say they were fashioned with the promise land in mind! The same must hold true in a spiritual promise land.

We were created to overcome. I am convinced that we would die naturally and spiritually, if we never encountered another test or trial. I'm sure you have read newspaper accounts of famous people who have committed suicide and we can't imagine why. They seem to have everything a person could desire, love, money, power and a reputation for being the absolute best in their field. They have entered a flat land, no mountains to climb and no rivers to cross. There is - no more struggle.

So they blow their brains out! Why? Because we don't know how to live without a challenge. That's why I felt so devastated as I sat on those steps outside my new home in Ohio. I was used to climbing mountains but there was none to climb. I was used to crossing over rivers but there was not a river in sight. I had come to a flat land and it was killing me!

As the seed of Abraham, the father of the faithful, we have inherited a Spiritual Land of mountains, rivers and valleys. But, Fear Not! We acquired the spiritual ability to conquer all obstacles the moment we are born-again. The problems that arise thereafter result from our perception of that inheritance. The majority of Christians do not view spiritual mountains, rivers or valleys very kindly!

4 LOOKS CAN BE DECEIVING

Valley, "An elongated lowland between ranges of mountains, hills or other uplands, often having a river or stream running along the bottom." *Keep in mind that a natural valley is a replica of a spiritual valley.*

A valley is a sheltered place, protected from strong winds and severe cold by the mountains surrounding it. The river that winds along the mountain bottom testifies that life-sustaining water is running from the mountaintop into the valley. Vegetation and all manner of life abound in the valley. Doesn't seem so bad does it?

And yet, in a Christian's mind, the valley is a "hated" place. That's how we look at it. To us, it is a dry, deserted and God-forsaken place void of life and happiness. That's how we perceive it. And what we see is what we get!

Therefore, we have come to hate the valley. But that mind-set creates a huge problem because God is not on the mountaintop any longer. He is in the valley. In the Old Testament we learn that the Israelites had to go up on Mount Sinai to commune with God. In the New Testament, God came down to man.

Song of Solomon 2:1, *"I am the rose of Sharon, and the lily of the valleys."*

Saint John 1:14, *"And the Word was made flesh, and dwelt among us,..."*

God has not just come down for a visit; He is firmly rooted in the valley. So if Jesus is in the valley, why is that the one place on earth we hate to be?

In this life we will have tests and trials until the day we die. That is a fact of life. For no matter how we pray or grow spiritually, we will NEVER get to a place where we don't have to go through or get over, something. I'm talking about real, physical, everyday problems and situations we have to deal with. And we must lean to deal with natural problems one way, spiritually.

Ephesians 6:12, *"For we wrestle not against flesh and blood, but against principalities, against powers, against the rulers of the darkness of this world, against spiritual wickedness in high places."*

I remember where I was and what song I was listening to when that truth finally entered and took up residence in my brain. I had just put gas in my car and was waiting to pull out of the station when a song came on the radio that I liked. I had heard it before but this time I really listened to the words. And then I started screaming, out loud!

The song was, "He Covers Me", by Steve Camp, and the chorus goes like this;

And though the trials never end,
I've learned to take them as my friends,
but for now He covers me".

I screamed at the radio, "What did you say, what did you say?" You see, somewhere in the back of my mind I thought that someday I would be saved enough or mature enough spiritually that I wouldn't have to go through or get over, anything else. And I certainly didn't think of my tests and trials as friends. They were my worst enemies or so I perceived.

After the message of that song convicted my spirit, God taught me a powerful lesson. He first reminded me of how I had loved to climb the mountains around my childhood home. Then He asked, "When you walked outside and there were mountains all around, did you get scared and say, I can't take anymore, I hate mountains?"

"No, Lord," I answered.

"How did you feel about the mountains?" He questioned.

"I thought they were beautiful and I couldn't wait to climb them," I replied.

"Why can't you look at your spiritual mountains that way?" He asked. "Why do you always look at them negatively? If you look at them in a different way, you will handle them in a different way!"

What you see *IS* what you get!

God helped me to see that we needed to change how we view mountains, rivers and valleys. As I said before, tests and trials will always be with us. Usually, things that stick by you are called Friends. That's why Steve Camp sang, "I've learned to take them as my friends." He changed his mind about how he saw his tests and trials. Someone once said, "I get by with a little help from my friends" and the Bible tells us that Jesus is a friend that sticks closer than a brother. We have some other friends that stick real close too – tests and trials! Because when mama and all the rest of the family, your mall-running buddies and even your closest companions forsake you, tests and trials will be there. You can count on them. And isn't that the definition of a true friend?

That's why King David said, "I will lift up mine eyes unto the hills, from whence cometh my help." The hills reminded him of all the previous mountains he had climbed and because he had conquered those, he had faith to believe he could climb the ones in front of him. Once known enemies had become helpful friends. It's all in how you look at it.

The issue is not the mountains, rivers and valleys in our lives; it's our perception of them. **Perception** means, "The act or process of perceiving, any insight or knowledge arrived at by perceiving. To **Perceive** means, "To become aware of something through the senses, see, hear, feel, touch or smell. To come to understand, apprehend with the mind." (Funk & Wagnall's Standard Desk Dictionary)

In the natural world we see mountains and rivers as obstacles and valleys as the lowest point on earth. So we take our sight (perception) of the natural realm and transfer it to the spiritual realm and we see our tests, trials and spiritual valleys the same way, negatively. And negative sight brings negative reactions.

But what would happen if we changed our outlook? What if we had a paradigm shift and our thinking turned upside down, hated places became places of power, enemies became friends and negative perceptions became positive sights? We would give the devil a headache the size of Texas, that's what would happen! However, before we can correct our misconception of mountains, rivers and valleys, we need to know where that false perception came from.

5 THE POWER OF PERCEPTION

Psalm 23:16, *"The Lord is my shepherd; I shall not want. He maketh me to lie down in green pastures: he leadeth me beside still waters. He restoreth my soul: he leadeth me in the paths of righteousness for his name's sake Yea, though I walk through the valley of the shadow of death, I will fear no evil: for thou art with me; thy rod and thy staff they comfort me. Thou preparest a table before me in the presence of mine enemies: thou anointest my head with oil; my cup runneth over. Surely goodness and mercy shall follow me all the days of my life: and I will dwell in the house of the Lord for ever."*

    A few years back I was at work loading a machine with ham slices and minding my own business when, *"yea, though I walk through the valley of the shadow of death"*, swept forcefully and unexpectedly through my mind. Then God asked, "Now what do you notice about that scripture?" I really wanted to reply with something intelligent and spiritual but I had no idea what He was talking about. He knows me well, so He went ahead and gave me the answer.
    "David named his valley!"
    It hit me like the proverbial ton of bricks. You only put a

name to something that is *important*! As Christians, we always want to be on the mountaintop. We don't want any other part of the mountain nor are we interested in the experience of the climb, we just want to get to the tippy-top. But David did not even mention a mountain in Psalms 23 and there had to have been mountains around somewhere if there was a valley. He recognized the importance of the valley.

A Valley is a depression of the earth's surface; therefore, it is naturally lower than the land around it. When we are in a spiritual valley, we feel like we are in a pit that God with all of His power cannot get us out of. We can't imagine anything good coming out of a valley experience but we are about to learn that the place that has been hated, dreaded and feared is really…a place of power.

The Lord is our Shepherd In The Valley. He protects us and provides for all of our needs In The Valley. Our soul is restored as we walk beside still waters and rest in green pastures In The Valley. The Lord comforts us and drives away all fear In The Valley. With His rod and His staff, He destroys our adversaries and guides our steps In The Valley. God prepares a table for us in the presence of our enemies In The Valley. He anoints us with oil and equips us to do the work He has created us for In The Valley. All of these wondrous things take place – IN THE VALLEY!

Somehow we get the idea that David was talking about a horrible place when He wrote parts of the 23rd Psalm. We love verses one through three but verse four sounds like it came from a different book. Verses five and six restore our hope but it is verse four that sticks in our minds. However, David was talking about the same place, *the valley*, in all six verses. The valley never changed, our perception of it did. All because of twelve little words, *Yea, though I walk through the valley of the shadow of death*!

Picture yourself walking in a valley. Walk to the west and allow the crispness of the morning air to wash fresh across your face. Move to the south and breathe in the fragrant aroma of dew-dampened grass and blooming wildflowers. Head towards the north and listen to the music that's being played down a lazy, winding riverbed. And finally, turn to the east where night shadows are being chased away by a rising, golden sun. Is there any problem in that valley? NO. There is no problem until a mountain or a river blocks your pathway, something you have to get over or go through. So, why does the valley get such a bum rap?

Perception and a negative mindset.

The spirit of negativism has a strong hold in the house of the living God. Do the following statements sound familiar? Something bad will happen before something good happens. The bottom will fall out from under us the minute God starts to bless us. The devil will attack us as soon as we step into the call God has on our lives. Regrettably, God's people have become accustomed to thinking negatively. The moment we see or hear the words *valley*, *shadow* or *death*, it produces a negative mindset but God hates negative thinking!

What is the number one reason we need to change our

perception of our spiritual valleys? *Time!* We will be spending much of our spiritual lives in a valley of some sort, so if we don't change our attitude about that "hated" place, the time we spend there will be miserable.

Isaiah 40:4, *"Every valley shall be exalted, and every mountain and hill shall be made low..."*

Exalt your valley! Lift it up in your mind to a place of importance and power. Get rid of that mountaintop obsession and make the valley your goal. Perceive it differently and you will begin to see the valley for what it really is, your power station!

6 WHERE POWER RESIDES

Power: "The right, ability, or capacity to exercise control; legal authority. Strength or force actually put forth. A mental or physical faculty. Any form of energy available for doing work." (Funk & Wagnall's Standard Desk Dictionary)

What makes a place powerful? The existence of a power source.

For power to be powerful, it must be in a place and it must be connected to a power source. Think of the home you live in. The electrical wiring throughout the house brings power into it. Without a doubt, power resides in that place. But if an electrical cord is not plugged into an outlet, you have no manifestation of power.

Another example, a foreign king or queen has power to rule in their own country but has no governing authority when visiting the United States. When they leave their homeland, they step out of their place of power and disconnect themselves from their power source.

The purpose of this book is to focus our attention on a place of absolute and limitless power; a Spiritual Valley. That statement probably goes against every thought we have had about our own valleys. Our valleys are the lowest point in our spiritual lives, a living hell on earth and the nightmare we have to endure to get to the mountaintop. Seldom, if ever, do we recognize it as a place of supreme power.

John 1:1,14, *"In the beginning was the Word, and the Word was with God, and the Word was God. And the Word was made flesh, and dwelt among us,..."*

St. Matthew 28:18, *"And Jesus came and spake unto them, saying, All power is given unto me in heaven and in earth."*

If you look at the distance between heaven and earth, in parallel, they become a mountain and a valley. God left His mountaintop, heaven, and came to live with us in a valley, earth. And because of His presence, *all power* resides in that place.

Power is given to a person who has gone to *the* place.

A mountain climber does not receive the power or ability to climb Mt. Everest from the top of that mountain. He gains power in the valley beneath Mt. Everest. He exercises his body so that he can endure the struggle of the climb. He charts his course and plots the best route up the mountain. He evaluates how much food, clothing and equipment will be needed for the journey. He does all of his preparing in the valley.

Likewise, an astronaut prepares for flight in a valley called Earth. There he checks and double checks the spaceship that will carry him to his moon mountaintop. He learns how to walk and work in gravity-free conditions by going through various simulations. He refines his piloting skills and familiarizes himself with the mechanics of his spacecraft. He makes sure his spacesuit is airtight and his oxygen tank full. The smallest detail is planned in the valley.

The mountain climber and the astronaut recognize the value of the valley. It is where they are trained, equipped and empowered to reach their destination. They have also faced one other fact, they will spend a whole lot more time in the valley preparing for their journeys, than they will spend on their "mountaintops" savoring their victories.

Unfortunately, I know very few Christians who want to stay in a valley. Maybe that's why we are not as powerful as we could be. We hate our place of preparation so we leave before we are trained, equipped and empowered to reach our destination.

Several years ago NASA launched a spaceship which exploded within minutes, killing all aboard. A piece of equipment, which should have been fixed on the ground, malfunctioned. In hindsight, we know that those astronauts were dead before they ever left the earth. Dead because they didn't use the valley to make sure everything was working properly for the trip up their mountain.

We seldom die climbing a mountain. We usually die in the valley. Why? Because we don't recognize the valley for what it is, God's ordained place of power. God is not backwards! *He placed the valley at the foot of a mountain for a reason.* There is no way to even get to a mountain to climb, unless you go through a valley. That applies to both the natural and the spiritual mountain.

God uses the valley to empower us for the climb up our spiritual mountains and that preparation takes Time. But time is the one thing we do not want to spend in a valley. A few months ago one of our Sunday School teachers taught a lesson entitled, "Intimacy In The Valley". Finally, someone had seen the importance of the valley and they were going to share that insight! However, as the weeks passed I noticed a prevailing attitude in the class. Even though the teacher had talked about being intimate with God in the valley, most of the class members were still saying, "I can't wait to get out of the valley!"

My question is – how can you be intimate with someone you keep running away from? Imagine this scenario, your spouse hires a babysitter, closes up the office and whisks you away to a special, intimate place. Now, they have gone to a lot of trouble and money to make sure that their time with you is not interrupted. In this private place they open themselves up to you as never before, sharing their hopes and dreams for the future. One thing leads to another and they seek intimacy with you. They kiss and caress you, telling you over and over again how much you mean to them. And you look into their love-filled eyes and say; "Can we hurry up and get this over with? I have somewhere I want to go."

How do you think your spouse would feel in this situation? Most likely, heartbroken!

Well, how do you think God feels when He has purposely fashioned a place where He can be intimate with you and you can't wait to get out of it? Heartbroken! God created the valley so that He would have a place where He could be alone with you. It was His desire to meet you there from time to time and reveal Himself and His plans to you. Needless to say, if you hate being there, you are not going to be very receptive to God's love nor the directives He gives you in the valley. And without God's help it will be impossible for you to climb your spiritual mountains or cross your spiritual rivers.

Power is gained from our valley experiences when we change our perception of our "hated" place. But that will not happen until we shake off our mountaintop mentality. Sometimes, God is forced to use an enemy to show us that He is not only God on the mountaintop but also God in the valley.

7 GOD OF THE VALLEY

The Bible has one great story after another declaring the victories of God. One of my favorites is found in I Kings Chapter 20. It is the account of Ahab, king of Israel, and his battle with Ben-Hadad, the king of Syria.

Samaria, the capital of the Northern Kingdom of Israel, was situated on a hill that was three hundred feet high. There, Ahab and his wife, Jezebel, ruled over a powerful kingdom. However, after the prophet Elijah commanded the rain to stop, a three-year famine ensued and the land became impoverished. Ben-Hadad, king of Syria, took advantage of the weakened kingdom and chose that time to bring his army against Samaria.

After Samaria was besieged, Ben-Hadad commanded Ahab to give up his wives, his children and all of his silver and gold. Hoping to save his life and spare the city from being looted, Ahab agreed. But the king of Syria was not satisfied and demanded that Ahab let his soldiers enter Samaria and take what they wanted from it. Ahab went to the elders of Israel and told them about the demands Ben-Hadad had made. They advised Ahab to refuse the king of Syria's demands and he did so. Upon hearing this, Ben-Hadad ordered his army to fight against Samaria.

About this time, a prophet came to King Ahab and asked him if he had seen the multitude that had come against Israel. The prophet then told Ahab that God was going to deliver the army of Syria into his hands. Following the directions of God, the famine-weakened army of Israel defeated the army of Syria with a great slaughter. However, Ben-Hadad, the King of Syria managed to escape. The prophet came back to Ahab and told him to prepare his army because the king of Syria would return for war again in the spring of the next year.

After their defeat, the servants of Ben-Hadad, King of Syria, came to him with advice. They said, "Their gods (Israel's) are gods of the hills. Therefore, they are stronger than we, but if we fight against them in the plain (valley), surely we will be stronger than they." The Syrians believed that the outcome of the battle depended on the strength of the *gods* of the opposing forces, instead of the strength of the armies themselves. They also believed that a deity's power extended over a limited area of that god's jurisdiction only. So, they believed that the God of Israel only had power over the place where His people lived, the Hill City of Samaria.

Ben-Hadad's servants suggested that he reconstruct an army like the one he had lost, horse for horse, chariot for chariot, and then fight the army of Israel in the plain. He followed their advice and led his army to battle against Israel at Aphek, an area around the Jordan Valley. The Bible points out that the camp of Israel was like two little flocks of goats, while the Syrians filled the countryside.

Again, a prophet went to Ahab with a word from God. He said, "Thus saith the Lord, Because the Syrians have said, The Lord is God of the hills, but he is not God of the valleys, therefore will I deliver all this great multitude into thine hand, and ye shall know that I am the Lord."

The armies of Israel and Syria encamped opposite one another other for seven days and on the seventh day, the battle began and Israel slew one hundred thousand foot soldiers of the Syrian army in *one* day. The remaining Syrians, about twenty-seven thousand, fled into the city of Aphek where they were destroyed when God caused a wall to fall on them. Israel had total victory, because God was God in their valley!

Remember that the Syrians believed that the outcome of the battle depended on the strength of the gods of the opposing forces instead of the strength of the armies themselves. In other words, if Ben-Hadad and his army had known *anything* about the God of Israel, they would have known better than to fight against Samaria! Their resulting defeat leads many of us to believe that Ben-Hadad was not too smart. He foolishly underestimated the power of God. We, in turn, have become smug about Israel's victory over Syria. After all, Israel was God's chosen people. We have even looked down our noses at the advice of Ben-Hadad's servants who told him that Israel's God was not God of the valley.

But, how many times have we said, maybe in a different way, that God is not God of our valleys? How many times have we been on the mountaintop, acknowledging the power of our God, only to find ourselves feeling hopeless in the next valley? How many times have we found ourselves in a situation/valley so devastating that we fail to believe God can deliver us from it? How many times have we let God know that we don't believe that He is as much God in our valley as He is on our mountaintop?

God proved to the Syrians and to the Israelites, that He is even more God in the valley. Of course, we know that God can never be more or less than God. But He became more in their eyesight after their victory in the Jordan valley. He showed His people that He was master over every situation, no matter how hopeless it seemed.

I hope that by this time you have a better appreciation of the valley. I know I do. And now that we have identified the valley for the place of power that it is we can face our mountains and rivers with a different perspective. And that different perception will guarantee Victory!

8 TEST OR TRIAL

Test: "An examination made for the purpose of proving or disproving some matter in doubt." **To Test**: "To subject to a test or trial; try. Subjection to conditions that disclose the true character of a person or thing in relation to some particular quality." **Trial**: "The act of testing or proving by experience or use. The state of being tried or tested, as by suffering: hour of trial." (Funk & Wagnall's Standard Desk Dictionary) <u>A Test is a spiritual mountain you must climb. A Trial is a spiritual river you must cross.</u>

When you have a mountain test you will be surrounded with trouble on every hand. Have you ever seen a mountain sitting out in a valley all by itself? Me neither! There will always be more than one mountain facing you at any given time but that doesn't mean you have to climb them all at the *same* time.

A river trial on the other hand will be solitary. It will be a focused attack by the devil on one area of your life, God's personal word to you. The attack comes to make you doubt what God has said, because if you don't believe God's word, you can never receive the thing He has promised.

9 GRAVITY OR PRESSURE

While God was talking to me about mountain climbing one day, He asked, "What are you fighting against as you climb upwards?" "Gravity," I answered. "What is gravity?" He inquired. When I didn't answer right away, He said, "Gravity is *nothing more* than glorified pressure. That is the negative way to think about it. Now, what is glorified pressure?" My silence led Him to respond again. "Glorified pressure is pressure I *allow* you to be put under for my glory. That is the positive way to look at it."

Gravity: (Physics) "The natural force of attraction exerted by a celestial body such as Earth upon objects at or near its surface, tending to draw them toward the center of the body." (The American Heritage Dictionary) In other words, gravity is what keeps us from falling off of the face of the earth!

Pressure: "The application of continuous force by one body upon another that it is touching, compression. (Physics) Force applied uniformly over a surface, measured as force per unit of area. A compelling or constraining influence, such as a moral force, on the mind or will." (The American Heritage Dictionary)

Force: "Power exerted on any resisting person or thing. (Physics) Anything that changes or tends to change the state of rest or motion in a body." (Funk & Wagnall's Standard Desk Dictionary)

When we deal with gravity, it is the force trying to hinder our motion/movement as we climb up our mountain. It is fighting to hold us down. Pressure is the force that tries to change us, our beliefs and our position, as we cross a flooded river. Suffice it to say, as we climb our spiritual mountains and cross our spiritual rivers there is a determined force against us.

How we perceive that force will determine what we will obtain from it. If we look at it negatively that force will become our undoing. If we look at it positively and learn how to harness it, that force will become our greatest asset. Again, it's all in how you look at it.

Do you remember the show "Star Trek," with Captain Kirk and his crew of futuristic astronauts? There were many times when their ship, The Enterprise, got trapped in an alien ship's tractor beam or the gravitational pull of another planet. They would have to use all of their power and fuel just to break free. The result; once loosed the same force (gravity) that had held them captive, now hurled them into a new and previously unattainable dimension.

What about another oldie but goodie, "Voyage to the Bottom of the Sea?" Captain Nelson and his crew were on what was at that time a state-of-the-art submarine. Trouble (pressure) came at them in numerous forms, warring countries, aliens, undersea earthquakes and countless other life-threatening situations, not to mention the constant force they endured from the water they traveled through. During those *pressing* times, Captain Nelson gave one command – Dive! Dive! And the same pressure that took them deeper always brought them out on top.

When we are climbing our mountain tests we become "astronauts." We have to fight against the gravitational pull of the cosmos, the world, so that we can reach a peak of spirituality that we have not attained before. When we're crossing our river trials we become "deep-sea divers." We go from one level of pressure to another, our trials forcing us into a deeper relationship with God.

I'm reminded of what an astronaut and a deep-sea diver never leave home without, their pressure suits. These special suits were designed to help them withstand *pressure changes*. The Lord designed such an outfit for you and me. It works just as well when we're struggling against gravity while climbing our spiritual mountain as it does when we're striving to withstand pressure during the crossing of our spiritual river.

Ephesians 6: 13-18, *"Wherefore take unto you the whole armour of God, that ye may be able to withstand in the evil day, and having done all, to stand. Stand therefore, having your loins gird about with truth, and having on the breastplate of righteousness; And your feet shod with the preparation of the gospel of peace; Above all, taking the shield of faith, wherewith ye shall be able to quench all the fiery darts of the wicked. And take the helmet of salvation, and the sword of the Spirit, which is the word of God: Praying always..."*

As we forge onward learning more about our spiritual mountains and rivers there are a few things we need to keep in mind. God designed the valley as a special and intimate place for us. It is where He taught us through life-lessons how to overcome the obstacles that block our way. Then God designed a pressure suit that allows us to withstand any outside force we meet as we embark on our spiritual odysseys. We have been equipped and empowered, let the journey begin.

10 THE PRINCIPLE THING

St. Matthew 18:18, *"Verily I say unto you, Whatsoever ye shall bind on earth shall be bound in heaven: and whatsoever ye shall loose on earth shall be loosed in heaven."*

If you cannot accomplish something in the natural world it cannot be accomplished in the spiritual world! That principle might sound very limiting but actually, just the opposite is true. A few hundred years ago most men would have agreed that it was impossible to travel to the moon. Today, it is possible. Several centuries ago it was not thought possible that organs could be taken from one human and put into another. Today, it is possible. We don't know what tomorrow holds, what wondrous things might be accomplished. The prospects are limitless! And if it has been done or can be done in the natural world, it can be done in the spiritual world. This is a Divine principle.

Principle: "A comprehensive and fundamental law, doctrine, or assumption. A rule or code of conduct, a beginning, a primary source, an origin." (The Merriam Webster's Collegiate Dictionary) So if a principle is a law, what is a law?

Law: "A rule of conduct, recognized by custom or decreed by formal enactment, considered as binding on the members of a community or nation. An authoritative rule or command, Divine will, command or precept. A body of rules having such divine origin."

Oftentimes, we talk about God's laws and principles as though they were synonymous. However, there is one main difference between them. A law is usually relegated to time and place. It can be and often is, changed by God. A principle, on the other hand is a law that does not change. It is fundamental, the original source of God's teachings.

The principle, which is also known as a doctrine, comes first. Then laws are given for direction and instruction in that doctrine. For example, in the Old Testament a blood sacrifice had to be brought to the temple at certain times of the year to make atonement for the sins of the people. It was an ongoing, yearly process. In the New Testament, Jesus shed His blood once, for all people. The fact that salvation required a blood sacrifice was a principle, a fundamental, unchangeable doctrine. How that sacrifice was offered was a law and that law changed from the Old Testament to the New Testament.

I said all of that to say this – *you can only do in the spiritual realm what can be done in the natural realm.* That is a Divine principle and it cannot be changed. Since the rest of the book is tightly woven around that principle, I thought we might need a few Biblical examples to cement it into our minds.

In Isaiah 38, a king named Hezekiah was seriously ill. The Lord sent the prophet Isaiah to Hezekiah to tell him to set his house in order because he was going to die.

Hezekiah turned his face to the wall and prayed so passionately that God extended his life for fifteen more years. God also promised Hezekiah that He would defend and deliver the city of Judah out of the hand of the king of Assyria. Then the Lord gave Hezekiah a sign to prove that He would keep His promise. In those days, they used a sundial to tell time. A pole was placed so that its shadow traveled down a staircase gradually to show the passing of the hours. God told Hezekiah that He would cause the shadow to move *backwards* ten degrees, a miraculous occurrence in which God proved that He was able to keep His promises and Hezekiah regained lost time.

Have you ever felt like you have lost time spiritually with God and wished you could get it back? Well, you can. A precedent was set in the natural realm when God forced time to move backwards for Hezekiah. We can now take that natural precedent and apply it in the spiritual world.

In St. John 11, a man named Lazarus was sick unto death. He had two sisters, Mary and Martha, and they were all close friends of Jesus. The sisters sent word to Jesus after their brother became ill, hoping that he would come and heal His friend, but Jesus did not come and Lazarus died. By the time Jesus showed up in Bethany, Lazarus had been in the grave for four days. Mary and Martha, both somewhat upset with Jesus, criticized Him for not coming sooner to save their brother. Jesus asked where they had buried Lazarus and when He arrived at the cave, He commanded that they take away the stone from the entrance to the tomb. Then He said, "Lazarus, come forth."

And a man who had gone through the processes of death walked out of the tomb alive and whole.

God used Lazarus to set a precedent in the natural world; dead men can live again. Therefore, a person who has died spiritually can be brought back to life spiritually. As someone who has been there and done that I can testify to that fact!

The Bible gives many other examples of things that can be done or have been done in this natural world. Moses and the children of Israel crossed a natural Red Sea. Joshua commanded a natural sun and moon to stand still in the valley of Ajalon until Israel's enemies were destroyed. Three Hebrew boys, Shadrach, Meshach and Abednego, walked around in a natural fiery furnace. David fought against and destroyed a natural giant and the list goes on and on. Precedents have been set in the natural world; therefore, those same feats can be accomplished in the spiritual world.

11 ONE MOUNTAIN AT A TIME

The foundation has been laid; we are equating our spiritual tests with natural mountains. And a principle has been established, we only can do in the spiritual world what has been done or what can be done in the natural world.

Look around. What do you see? Mountains on every side, tests on every hand? Financial worries, family issues, physical ailments, spiritual deadness; everything is coming against you at once. You try to pass every test and climb every mountain at the same time but you fail. Why? I don't know about yours but my legs are not very long. There is *no way* I could straddle two natural mountains at the same time! And I'm pretty sure you can't either. And if you can't climb more than one mountain at a time in the natural world, why would you think that God would expect you to climb two or three mountains at the same time in the spiritual world? That would be against His principles.

But mountains surround you and the tests are very real, so the question really is, since you can only climb *one* at a time, which mountain/test has come between you and God? Has a financial crisis caused you to doubt God's ability to provide for you? Has a relationship caused a rift between you and God? Has an illness caused you to be angry with

God? No matter how many mountains are facing you, you only have to climb the one that has come between you and the lover of your soul!

When God brings about a test or allows the devil to bring one, that test is on purpose for one reason, there is a lesson to be learned. So, before you take a step, ask God to show you which mountain/test He wants you to conquer today. Because if there are four mountains facing you and it is only possible to climb one of them at a time, it is very important to be headed up the right mountain! For instance, if God intended to teach you steps to financial deliverance and you are forging your way up Mount Lust, you are not going to get out of your financial bondage. More importantly, the Bible says that the steps of a good man are ordered, (ordained, set in concrete) by the Lord. If God has prepared your way up Mount Finance and you are on another mountain, you are on your own!

One of my favorite, old gospel songs is, "Won't It Be Glory." It's about what we will say to God when we get to heaven. Part of the chorus goes like this,

"I'm going to sit down beside sweet Jesus,
tell Him all about my trouble,
tell Him how I made it over, climbing
up the rough side of the mountain,
on my way to the crystal fountain,..."

I was singing that song one day and I kept repeating one line over and over again; *climbing up the rough side of the mountain*. I wanted God to know that the mountain He had given me to climb had been an extremely rough one! Well, when God got tired of me complaining, He said, "You had better learn to thank me for the rough side."

Immediately, my mind went back to a TV show I had seen where a group of climbers were scaling a mountain of smooth rock. As they were climbing, they had to stop and chisel out places in the rock to put anchors in to secure their ropes. Every handhold and every foothold had to be cut out before they could proceed up the mountain. It was a smooth-sided mountain but it was much harder to climb because they had to create their own path.

Then God said, "The mountain I prepared for you might have seemed bumpy and jagged but that's because I went before you and paved the way. I twisted Earth to form places for your feet to rest during the journey. I bent rocks and cemented them into place so you would have a safe handhold. I anchored you with my word and held you secure with chords of love. You never had to worry about falling while you climbed because your steps were ordered by me." Thank You God!

For a moment, let's go back to our spiritual valley. We can spend time there now without fear knowing that it is the place where God empowers us to overcome ALL THINGS. As we walk along that valley looking at the surrounding mountains, one question occupies our minds, which mountain has God ordained for us to climb at this time?

12 THE PURPOSE OF A SHADOW

Purpose: "An idea or ideal kept before the mind as an end of effort or action design, aim. A settled resolution and determination." **On Purpose** means, "To have the intention of doing or accomplishing something." (Funk & Wagnall's Standard Desk Dictionary) **Shadow**: "The rough image cast by an object blocking rays of illumination. An imperfect imitation or copy, shelter or protection, a constant companion." (The American Heritage Dictionary)

One day I was depressed and worrying about my financial situation. I was going through a rough period where I only had a few dollars from week to week to buy food, gas or anything else that was needed. Suddenly, I had a light bulb moment! I thought, I'm in a valley and there are mountains all around but since money is my biggest worry, I need to climb Mount Finance. God, who heard my thoughts said, "Oh, is that what you're supposed to do? Maybe you should be still and know that I am God. Maybe you should be climbing *Be Still Mountain!*"

I had picked out the mountain/test that had been troubling me the greatest but it wasn't the one God wanted me to climb at that time. God helped me through that season of lack and then He began teaching me about the

Purpose of a Shadow.

A shadow is caused by things like mountains/tests, coming between us and the sun/Son. The good news is that God did not design the shadow to be a source of fear or dread. He purposed it to be a means of guidance and illumination. Let me clarify that thought further with *my version of the conception* of the 23rd Psalm.

Long, long ago, an aging and ailing King David went out walking early one morning and ended up in a valley bordered on all sides by lofty, majestic mountains. He had been in this valley many times before, but now looking around at the seemingly endless array of mountains, David became uneasy. He knew in his spirit that God had led him there for a reason but he wasn't sure why. Out of the corner of his eye David noticed a rather small mountain to the south of him. Turning to face it, the king smiled. Years ago, *Bear* Mountain had stood in his way but God had given him power to defeat that obstacle. Now he realized it was nothing more than a hill. To the west, a much larger mountain loomed and David, always respectful of God's anointed, gave an honorary bow to *Saul* Mountain. Funny how little that mountain seems after all of these years, he thought. Hesitantly, David turned to the north where *Absalom* Mountain, *Amnon* Mountain and *Joab* Mountain stood high and lifted up among a broad range of family mountains. I thought those would kill me, he remembered sadly. Finally, King David stepped to the east where an enormous mountain towered between him and a bright morning sun. A shadow created by the blocking of the sun's rays fell over the valley where David stood and he instantly felt an icy chill go up his spine. On the spot he named that place, "The Valley of the Shadow of Death," for he knew instinctively that the mountain facing him was *Death* Mountain. And he knew that he would either have to conquer it or die. Gathering all of his strength, the *apple of God's eye* battled his way up Mount Death, sat on the top victorious and then returned to the valley, healed and whole. As he left "The Valley of the Shadow of Death," David looked back at Death Mountain and from his spirit the 23rd Psalm arose.

A spiritual shadow has two purposes. It will let you know what is trying to come between you and God and it will illuminate the strategy of Satan. Because of a shadow, King David knew which mountain to climb. He didn't have to figure out what was trying to come between him and the sun/Son. The shadow guided him. Because of a shadow, David was able to perceive Satan's strategic plan to kill him through sickness. If God had not illuminated *Death* Mountain and if David had not climbed and successfully conquered it, he would have died.

So we can say that the purpose of a shadow is to darken the light. But God is light and Satan is full of darkness. Why would God allow the wicked one to obscure His light? When it's nice and bright outside we don't pay much attention to the sun, but let a little cloud get in the way of the sun's rays and we notice it immediately. We see the darkness, we feel the coldness. Sometimes it's hard for us to see that we have let things come between us and God, but a resulting shadow will spotlight the trouble. Only God could use a shadow to give light!

There is another side to the shadow principle. We know now that God creates a shadow for a purpose, *to show us the mountain we are to climb*. What happens, though, when the shadow is created by someone other than the Lord? One of my friends has several grown children and often her life is miserable because of what they are going through. She tries to help them out of their situations by giving them food, shelter, financial aid and advice, but all she's doing is creating another shadow. Remember, a shadow is caused by something coming between you and the sun/Son. So, let's say that God is allowing her children to go through some problems because He knows that those tests are what they *need* to bring them to Him. We all know that there were certain things that happened in our lives that sent us running to God. Without that broken heart, financial disaster, illness or the hitting rock bottom experience, many of us would not be saved now.

By preventing her children from going through various situations, my friend creates a shadow because now she is the one that is getting between them and the sun/Son. I'm not saying you shouldn't do what you can to help your kids. I'm just saying that it would be a good idea to ask God about His plans for their lives before you step in. Also, if you are spending all of your time, energy and resources helping your children or others overcome their mountains/tests, you won't have the time, energy, or resources to climb the mountain that God wants You to climb, like *Faith* Mountain, where you will find strength to believe that God is able to deliver all of your loved ones!

Reminder, In a natural valley you will be surrounded by very real and often intimidating, mountains. In a spiritual valley you will be surrounded by very real, often frightening tests. In either situation, you only have to climb *one* mountain/test at a time! That's all that God requires because that is all your physical or spiritual being can accomplish. And since you can only overcome one mountain/test at a time, nothing will be more important than being on the right mountain. Thankfully, God has given us a new friend and constant companion to highlight our pathway. May the Shadow be with you!

13 UP EXALTED MOUNTAINS

We have learned how to recognize the mountain we have to climb or the test we have to pass by looking for the shadow. Let's say that our lack of faith in God's ability to supply our needs has caused a problem in our relationship with Him. Therefore, Faith Mountain is the one that has caused a shadow by coming between us and the sun/Son. In order to regain our faith we must climb and conquer that mountain.

Where do we start? In our place of power; the Valley. First, let's back up in our valley until we can see the mountain from every angle. What we're really doing is distancing ourselves from the mountain/test so that we can look at it more objectively. If we stand too close to it we will only be able to see the mountain from one perspective, kind of like not being able to see the forest for the trees. The valley provides a panoramic view of the whole situation. This will enable us to chart our course. Will we start up the left side of the mountain, the right side, or march right up the middle? From what perception does God want us to see our spiritual test? Are we to see it as a thing of beauty that will bring glory to God when we have conquered it? Are we to see it as a lesson we need to learn before we get to the next valley? Are we to climb up on the paths of praise and worship or do we take the trails of prayer and fasting? We must use the valley to seek God for the wisdom and training needed to reach our destination.

Once we know what mountain test we are to climb and by what method, we need to decide what equipment to take with us. A positive mindset and a spirit of excitement are essential. If you are depressed about being in the valley you will find it hard to believe that you can reach the mountaintop. An attitude of thanksgiving and a cheerful heart are vital when climbing. God has been kind enough to highlight the problem with a shadow. That lets us know that He *greatly desires for us to succeed* in defeating the obstacle that created the shadow, which was our lack of faith. I can almost see Him now, cheering us on! Of course, when you go on any journey you need food and a compass, something to strengthen and guide you. We must take Jesus! He is the Word, the bread of life, the truth, the way and the life.

Thanks to the lessons we learned in the valley we have what is needed for the journey up our spiritual mountain. But before we head out let's take a look into our knapsack (heart), and see if we are carrying anything that we *don't* need. Astronauts and mountain climbers have this in common; they only take things that are absolutely indispensable on their trips. Because the more weight they carry the more energy they use and even a slight reduction in power could put an end to their expedition. I believe that one of the most important steps in preparing to climb a spiritual mountain is *getting rid of unnecessary, soul-draining weight.*

In the first chapter of this book I mentioned a situation in my life that had devastated me. It left me with a lot of anger, bitterness, an unforgiving spirit and a steadfast determination to never climb another spiritual mountain. Then came the day when God started encouraging me to climb again. I knew that He wanted me to climb Faith Mountain but I did not have the strength or desire to attempt that journey. I said, "Lord, I don't feel like climbing anymore. Maybe if this ordeal had happened when I was younger I could have bounced back from it but I'm tired. I can barely crawl let alone climb a mountain. There is no way I'm going *back* up there!"

If you don't pass your test by climbing your spiritual mountain all the way to the top on the first try, you will have to go through that test again. Why do we fail to reach the top? We lose Focus. We start up Mount Faith but then we look around at all of the other mountains in the valley. Mount Finance looks like it needs to be climbed immediately so we run down from Faith Mountain and start up Mount Finance. Bad mistake! I had climbed part way up Mount Faith before but never succeeded in reaching the summit. In school, if you don't complete the test you have to take it again. I was about to find out that the same law applied when climbing spiritual mountains.

God said, "Because you won't forgive you are weighed down with bitterness and anger. That's why you don't feel like climbing. Tell me, what do old mountain men do when they are weary and having a hard time making it up a mountain?"

"They cut a limb from a tree and make themselves a walking stick," I answered.

"I want you to get a walking stick," He admonished. "I want you to name that walking stick Forgiveness and I want you to walk with Forgiveness every day. Pretty soon you will start feeling lighter, after awhile you will be able to run and before long you will be climbing again."

The refusal or inability to Forgive is death to a spiritual mountain climber. There is no weight or burden that can equal its destructive might. It pulls at your mind, body and soul, leaving you incapable of upward movement. Even if you know what mountain/test God wants you to overcome and have charted your course and gathered your equipment, your efforts will be in vain if you do not let go of the things that are holding you down. You must Forgive.

I know what you're thinking. Easier said than done! But there is one approach that makes forgiveness possible, willingness. It is almost humanly impossible to forgive some of the wrongs that we have endured but if we're *willing* to forgive, God will do the work for us. Say you have an abscessed tooth. It is full of poison and that poison is being spread throughout your body, making you sick. The tooth needs to be extracted and for that you need a dentist. But the dentist does not come to your house to pull your tooth. You must be *willing* to go to him in order for him to remove the thing that is killing you. That's the way it is with God. You must take the first step and be willing to forgive. Then put yourself in His hands and let Him do the necessary work on your infected, unforgiving heart.

    Well, here you are, at the foot of your spiritual mountain. As you begin the climb there is one thing you must do, Stay Focused. Don't look around at the other mountains and by all means, don't look down. Set your face like flint and head for the top. As you reach higher altitudes the air will change and you might find it hard to breathe. Put on the pressure suit God designed for you and climb. Your legs might get tired and you may fear that you will fall. Reach out and grab hold of Jesus. He is the true vine and His love will anchor you. Continue to climb. After a while you will get to the point of no return. It will be easier to finish the climb than to turn around and go back down the mountain. Press on. Right about now your lungs feel like they're going to burst and your heart sounds like thunder in your ears. Climb. All of a sudden your fingers are grabbing air instead of dirt and your feet have found a solid foundation. You have just reached the top of your spiritual mountain! Take a few moments. Breathe in the fresh, sun-warmed air and enjoy the view. Place a memorial of thanksgiving there and give a shout of praise. You have successfully conquered the obstacle that was coming between you and God! There is only one thing left to do, return to the valley and get ready for the next mountain.

    Now, you just had one of two reactions to that last statement. If I have been successful in making you see the valley as a place of power, you won't mind leaving the mountaintop and going back to the valley. If I failed in my assignment, you shuddered and said, "I don't want to go back to the valley!" Tell the truth, which one was it? I pray you had the first reaction because – you really don't have a choice.

We have already discussed the fact that we will always have spiritual mountains to climb. So you knew before you started up your mountain that there would be a series of mountains after it. And the only way to get to another mountain is to come down from the one you're on, because you cannot, in the natural world or in the spiritual world, step from one mountaintop to another. That automatically places you in a valley. But what valley you end up in depends on which way you come down from the mountain. If you come down the same way you went up then you will be in the same valley as before, facing the same mountains. And who knows? God may have another mountain for you to climb in that valley. However, if you go down the opposite side of the mountain you will enter a different valley with a new set of mountains/tests. So while you're up there enjoying the view you might want to get some directions from God.

The Red Sea Experience

Walking, then running, sweat pouring down my back,
Looking over my shoulder, waiting for the enemy's attack.
My legs are failing and my knees are weak,
A safe, restful haven is all that I seek.
Fear propels me, forcing my tired body into moving,
The instinct for self-preservation is all that keeps me going.
Suddenly the mountains appear, one on each side,
Perhaps there is a place between them for me to hide.
Running past the mountains, my eyes search the land beyond,
And my heart almost stops beating, for now all hope is gone.

        Lying Before Me –The Red Sea!

I fall to my knees, admitting my defeat,
Then out of heaven a voice, so strong, so soft, so sweet.
"I will fight for you; you will not face the enemy's sword,
Rise Up, Be Still, and see the salvation of your Lord!
In this desperate situation there is humanly nothing you can do,
So rest in the arms of your Savior and I will carry you through.
Am I a man that I should lie?"
The waves seemed to shudder at the sound of His cry.
"Have I spoken and shall it not be?"
There was definite movement in the midst of my sea.
"No weapon formed against you shall destroy your life!"
The waters were cut asunder as if by some huge invisible knife.

As they stood upon an heap, listening to a voice only they heard,
I knew they had been wrenched apart by the power of His word!
Dry land appeared, a pathway in the midst of a cold, deadly sea,
And I walked across in Victory for my God truly delivered me!

    Lying Behind Me –The Red Sea!

14 THE RED SEA VS THE JORDAN

A **Sea** is, "A body of salt water of second rank more or less landlocked." (Merriam Webster's Collegiate Dictionary) A **River** is, "A natural stream of water of usually considerable volume, watercourse." (Merriam Webster's Dictionary) **Pressure** is, "the application of continuous force by one body on another that it is touching, compression." (The American Heritage Dictionary)

By the help of God I made it through my Red Sea experience without too many problems. But crossing my Spiritual Jordan was a different matter. So one day I asked the Lord, "Why am I having such a hard time getting over this river?" "Because there is a little more pressure involved," He answered. Then He broke it down for me. Remember, in a trial/river we experience Pressure.

A sea is a body of water partially or completely surrounded by land but the sea level is not higher at one end than at the other end. If it was all of the water would run out. Rivers run into and out of a sea but it basically stays level. Think of a bathtub filled with water. It is a body of water enclosed by a porcelain tub.

That means that if you were to divide the sea into two parts there would be as much water (pressure) on one side as on the other side. In the book of Exodus God promised that He would take the children of Israel out of the bondage of Egypt into a land flowing with milk and honey. That promise was based upon His word but the Red Sea stood in their way. God commanded Moses to raise his rod over the sea. It was then that God caused the sea to separate. It was actually His Word that made the pathway through the Red Sea because when God says you're coming out, *nothing* can stand in your way!

I can envision God, the Word, stepping into the midst of the Red Sea, legs fixed, arms stretched out to the sides. I can see the waters being separated and forced to the left and right as He extends His hands and pushes with - His little fingers! I can imagine a vast supply of ever-changing liquid being transformed into solid, immovable waves. I picture Him holding those waves high in the air, smiling down on His children as they walked through the Red Sea. And not once did God falter or lose His balance because there was the same amount of pressure on the right side of Him as there was on the left. And because He's God of course!

Crossing the Jordan River is a different story. At the Red Sea God taught Moses and the Israelites the principle of getting through a whole lot of pressure. The principle: *It is God's word that makes the pathway.* However, a new leader and a new congregation stood before the Jordan River and God was determined that they would practice a new principle.

In the third chapter of Joshua God's chosen people are preparing to cross the Jordan River. The priests, carrying

The Ark of the Covenant are commanded by Joshua to lead the way. As soon as the feet of the priests carrying the Ark were dipped into the overflowing river, Jordan divided. The priests then stood still in the Jordan River until all of the children of Israel passed over. The principle: *It is God's priest carrying the Word that creates the pathway.*

Exodus 19: 6, *"And ye shall be unto me a kingdom of priests, and an holy nation."*

1Peter 2:5, *"Ye also, as lively stones, are built upon a spiritual house, an holy priesthood,..."*

"Are you not my priest?" asked God.

"Yes, Lord," I answered.

Then He asked me what was in the Ark of the Covenant and I replied, "The Ten Commandments, Aaron's rod that budded and two quarts of manna." He was only interested in the tables of the law or The Word.

"I have given you a built-in-Ark," God said. "It's called a heart."

So we are the priests of God with the word of God in our hearts, what do we do next? Stand Still in our spiritual Jordan and watch it divide! As stated before a spiritual river is a *trial* not a test. On trial will be your faith in God's personal word to you. So if you want your spiritual Jordan to open up you had better be sure you heard from God. And you had better be sure you can stand on that word, no matter how much pressure you have to endure!

Here we go. We step into our spiritual Jordan, plant our feet firmly, stretch out our arms and push back the waters, but wait! Why do we feel so off balance? Why can't we keep our feet from slipping? Why do we feel like we're being overwhelmed? Because a river runs one way, downhill! That means that all of the water/Pressure is coming from one direction.

Naturally, and more to the point spiritually, what is a river trial? It is the greatest obstacle blocking the entrance into our promise land. For Israel, *It was also the last!*

Mount Hermon, with its snow covered peaks is over 9,000 feet above sea level. Four streams originating from there converge to create the Jordan, a swift, curving river that runs over two hundred miles before emptying into the Dead Sea. The Dead Sea is a salt lake located on the border between Israel and Jordan. Its shoreline is the *lowest point on the earth's surface,* averaging 1,300 feet below sea level. I guess you could say when Joshua and Company came to their point of crossover that they were in the valley of all valleys!

Let's see where pressure actually comes in. When I visited Niagara Falls in Canada one thing really surprised me. The river flowing into the falls was not very deep. I probably could have waded across it except for one little thing - pressure. And the closer you got to the mouth of the falls the greater the pressure became.

Joshua and the children of Israel crossed the Jordan River at Jericho, which is close to the mouth of the Dead Sea. Get the picture? They had to cross at the point where the water pressure was at its maximum. Not only that, they went across the Jordan at the time of harvest when the river was flooded. Pressure on Pressure! They had to walk through that pressure with the word, the promise of a new land that God had given them.

Once more we are equating water with pressure or force. Therefore, our spiritual trial/river is the thing that tries to force us to doubt God's word to us. And it is at the moment of harvest, when the promise is visible and within reach that we experience the most pressure!

In order to get through your spiritual river trial without being swept away by the pressure you must have absolute faith in God's word to you. Because it is a personal word, *no one* will be able to help you get over your Jordan. No one else heard what God said to you. Neither is anyone else *responsible* for what God said to you. You are the sole recipient of that word and it is up to you to carry it to the other side of your promise land.

In summary, God does not carry us over our spiritual rivers; we carry Him, (His Word). The only reason we have a problem getting over is because there is a little more pressure involved. Just remember, it is pressure God allows us to be put under for His glory!

Has not God been glorified for the way the Israelites gained entrance into their promise land? Will He not be glorified in your natural and spiritual family and among your friends and enemies when they see you successfully cross your spiritual Jordan? And is not that the reason for our existence to glorify God? Yes, Yes and YES!

15 PRESSURIZED SAINTS

Pressure changes things! That is one of the most important lessons I learned from the river that ran past my childhood home in Jumbo, West Virginia. To recap, a trial is a spiritual river we have to cross. The water running down that river causes pressure. This means that as we cross that river we are being pressurized.

Pressurize: "To apply pressure to, to design to withstand pressure. (Informal) To subject to excessive stress, strain or vexation." (The American Heritage Dictionary) The thing that caught my attention was the conflicting definitions. The first definition for pressurize is to apply pressure to something. The second definition means the thing that is having pressure applied to it has been designed to withstand that very pressure!

It reminds me of the quality tests they run on cars to evaluate their safety. Automobile manufacturers build cars to withstand high levels of stress or pressure on their frames in case of an accident. Then they turn right around and put them through crash tests to see if they will stand up to that pressure. In order for a car to pass the safety check it must be able to take a certain amount of pressure without caving in. *Notice*, the persons designing the car knew ahead of time how much pressure they would be putting that car under. They had to know that before they built the car to ensure that it would measure up to the standards of the safety tests.

Have you forgotten that God created you? And He is much more skillful, detail-oriented and design conscious than any automobile maker ever has been or ever will be. Your Maker designed you with the ability to withstand all the pressure you would have to go through in life *before* He let that pressure be applied!

Then how does pressure change you if you were built to withstand that pressure? It comes down to one variable; how you choose to let the pressure of your trial affect you. You can allow it to work for you or against you. When someone takes their trials and tragedies and uses them to become strong and successful they are authorizing pressure to work for them. On the other hand, when they choose to let trials ruin their lives they are consenting to pressure working against them. Ultimately, the variable is the choice they make.

When I tell you that I learned a *choice* lesson from a rock it might seem contradictory. How can an inanimate object teach us about making choices? Aside from human intervention a large river rock cannot become smaller or move from the right side of the riverbed to the left. There is only one thing that can change the size and position of that rock, pressure.

As a child I played in the river by our house as often as I could. I loved to jump from one rock to another all the way up and down the river. Because of those activities I was well acquainted with the size and location of the rocks in that river. After we moved to Ohio we would visit our old home at least once a year. But it was not until I was a lot older that I realized that the river was not like it had been when I was a child. One of my favorite big rocks was now near the bank of the river instead of in the middle. Others were farther down the river bed and some looked smaller. I know things always look different when you're a child but for the past several years I have taken picture after picture of that river and now I have proof of the changes that have been made!

One thing made those changes, pressure. Water forcing its way continually down the river eroded the surfaces of some of the rocks and changed their size and shape. Others were moved out of their places by floods. Even the contour of the river bed has changed.

That's how I learned a lesson from a rock. A rock has no say in the way pressure changes it. But We Do! I realized that I could let the pressure of the trials of this life shape me into being something other than what God purposed me to be, or I could place myself in God's hands and let that same pressure mold me into the person God designed me to be.

Pressure changes things! I learned that lesson by looking at the rocks in my beloved river and seeing the destructive results it had on those inanimate objects. I knew there had to be a positive counteraction. My definition of the Hoover Dam is, "pressure harnessed to produce power." That is what we have to do with the pressure that is applied during our trials, harness it and make it work for our good. God never wants the pressure He allows us to be under to work against us. He intended for it to make us crash-proof.

16 ACROSS IMPASSIBLE RIVERS

Some states have earthquakes, some have tornadoes and others have hurricanes. West Virginia has flash floods. A few days of rain will cause lazy, little streams to become swollen, raging torrents. Our family went down home a few years ago but I was disappointed when we got there because there was hardly any water in the river. The next day it rained and the river came up a little. The following day it rained all day and all night. By the time I got up the next morning the river was as high as the new cement bridge the neighbors had put in and it was starting to come into the yard. During the night I had heard a lot of loud, pounding noise from the rocks rolling down the now raging river. I don't think I have ever seen it that high or that wild. And that was with only a couple days of rain.

Like Joshua and the children of Israel we will have to cross our river/trial when it is flooded. During the Red Sea crossing the waters backed up and they went through on dry ground. However, because God has a lesson to teach us in our spiritual Jordan we will have to walk across while the pressure of our trial is washing over us. When a river is flooded it becomes muddy and impossible to see through. Therefore, we can't see where to put our feet so we don't know where the next step will take us. I always watched where I stepped when playing in our river because I didn't want to step into a "drop off". One minute the water would be up to my knees and the next step it could be to my waist and I couldn't swim!

If the water is muddy in our personal Jordan we won't be able to tell where the "drop off" is, and *nothing* takes you off balance as fast as going from one level of water (pressure) to another without warning. So how do we keep our balance as we walk through a flooded, spiritual river, especially when we're having a hard time seeing where to step? The best way is by equal distribution of the treasure or promise of God that we are carrying.

You cannot keep your balance if you believe what God has told you with your heart but your mind is not convinced. You will not stay balanced if your spirit is willing to believe and follow God into your promise but your flesh is weak. Body, soul and spirit must be in harmony, having complete faith in God's Word. That Word not only guarantees His promise, it becomes a lamp unto your feet and a light unto your pathway. And you will need both to avoid hidden "drop offs" as you cross your spiritual Jordan.

Total, unrelenting faith in God's word is the most important step in getting across your river trial. Build up your most holy faith during your valley experience. Use that time to confirm God's word by applying scripture, the Spoken Word and prayer. Remember, the children of Israel lodged on this side of Jordan for three days sanctifying themselves before they even started their journey. When they stepped to the banks of a flooded Jordan they were prepared and determined to go through.

Jeremiah 12:5, *"If thou hast run with the footman, and they have wearied thee, then how canst thou contend with horses? And if in the land of peace, wherein thou trustedst, they wearied thee, then how wilt thou do in the swelling of Jordan?"*

Changing your perception of your trial and the pressure accompanying it is imperative if you plan to end up on the other side of your spiritual Jordan. The pressure will either make you more determined than ever to believe what God has said or it will make you doubt that He has spoken to you at all. If you look at and use the pressure in a positive way it will be the force that propels you onto the shores of your promise land. If you look at and allow it to shape you negatively it will be the force that drives you back to where you first started from.

The only other thing you will need during the crossing of your river/trial is the pressure suit we talked about earlier. No matter what trial you are facing or how much pressure is being applied, if you are protected by your suit of armor you will endure without bending or breaking under the strain. You will be able to stand like the priests did as the children of Israel walked across a flooding Jordan. Stand, with the word of God ringing in your ears, cemented in your mind and soaring through your spirit. Stand, become more determined to make it over with every wave of pressure that assaults you. Stand, take that first step and then the next that leads you into your promise land.

When you get to the other side of your spiritual river...! You probably thought I was going to say give a shout of triumph like you did on the mountaintop. Sorry, no time for that right now. When you get to the other side of your trial you will either enter into a valley or you will immediately be faced with another mountain. Some rivers run down the middle of a valley, in which case you would go from valley-to-river-to-valley and on to a mountain. The river by my old home ran along the side of a mountain so while out playing I had to walk through the valley and cross the river to get to the mountain I wanted to climb. If that happens in your spiritual land you must prepare for both a test and a trial while in the valley. I call that *tribulation*! Let's pray it is a wide spiritual valley. It might take more time to walk through it but it will give you more time to prepare for what lies ahead. Maybe by now your mindset has changed and you won't mind spending time in the valley. Hopefully, you have come to love your "hated place."

17 THE CONCLUSION OF THE MATTER

Let me leave you with one more story about the valley just for fun. In II Kings:3, Jehoram, the evil son of Ahab was reigning as king over Israel in the capital of Samaria. During Ahab's reign Mesha the king of Moab had supplied him with thousands of lambs and rams but when Ahab died the king of Moab rebelled against Jehoram and refused to deliver more animals. King Jehoram decided to go to war against King Mesha and he asked Jehoshaphat, king of Judah, to help him. Jehoshaphat agreed and they traveled through the wilderness of Edom. There the king of Edom joined them and the three kings set out to subdue Mesha, king of Moab. But after journeying for seven days they came to a place where there was no water for the armies nor for the cattle that followed them.

Because of this calamity Jehoram, king of Israel, became convinced that the Lord had brought the three kings together to destroy them. Jehoshaphat, king of Judah, asked, "Is there not here a prophet of the Lord, that we may inquire of the Lord by him?" A servant replied that Elisha, the son of Shaphat, was there and the king of Judah said, "The word of the Lord is with him." The three kings asked the prophet Elisha what they should do because they were in a valley with no water. Because of his respect for Jehoshaphat, Elisha prayed for a word from God.

The Lord answered by way of Elisha, "Make this valley full of ditches."

1lKings 3:16-18, *"And he said, Thus saith the Lord, Make this valley full of ditches. For thus saith the Lord, Ye shall not see wind, neither shall ye see rain; yet that valley shall be filled with water, that ye may drink, both ye, and your cattle, and your beasts. And this is but a light thing in the sight of the Lord: He will deliver the Moabites also into your hand."*

Not only is the valley the most powerful place to be but supernatural deliverance comes when you really "dig" into it! My friends, love your Spiritual valley, climb your Spiritual mountains and cross your Spiritual rivers. Remember, God is waiting at the end of each journey.

18 A TUMBLE FROM THE TOP

I thought the book was finished, God had other ideas. I tried to publish, *Lessons Learned in Jumbo Valley*, but only received rejection notices. Disillusioned, I put the book away for the next eight years or so. Then a friend at church said you need to get that book done. I had almost forgotten that he had read part of it until he mentioned it. I asked another friend to read it and she loved it. Over the next several years others read it and loved it but it was still in my desk drawer. Then one day it hit me why I wasn't able to publish it, the story wasn't over. A few years ago during a visit to West Virginia I had an accident. I fell twenty-five feet off of a mountain while trying to take a picture! Thankfully, I survived and the *following* account of that miraculous deliverance is the perfect ending for, "Lessons Learned In Jumbo Valley".

I was on my back, arms stretched to the sides, hands trying to grasp something, anything that would break my fall. I knew I should be afraid even my *dreaming* mind told me this but somehow I wasn't. And then I came to a stop and a loud roaring began hammering at my unconscious mind. If I'm dreaming, I wondered, why am I not waking up in my bed? Then I heard my Aunt praying, asking Jesus to help me and I opened my eyes. "Aunt Esther, am I dreaming?" I asked? "No, honey," she said, "It's real. You fell." And then I remembered.

My Aunt and I had been sight-seeing at a remote, scenic area, The Falls of Hills Creek near Richwood, WV. A concrete walkway winds down to the first of three waterfalls and wooden steps along a mountain side take you to the second and third falls. We had just arrived at the first waterfall which measured 25 feet and I was trying to get a good picture, not an easy thing to do because of all the trees and brush. My Aunt said, "Why don't you come over here and lean on this tree and take a picture?" I looked at the tree, more like a *twig*, she was talking about and decided that wouldn't do. I could just picture it coming loose at the roots with all of my weight pushing against it. To my right, over the hillside was a rock and I thought, I can jump down on the rock and take a picture from there. I even reasoned that if I fell I would just grab hold of a nearby tree trunk until I got my balance. I was planning how I would fall before I fell! I'm sure God was warning me but I didn't listen. I had on a knee-length skirt, shoes with the heels out, with a camera around my neck and my purse hanging on my shoulder. A set up for disaster! As I leaned down to jump my aunt said, "Do you want me to take your purse?" I hesitated and at that moment I almost changed my mind. But I was already bent over and was afraid to try to get back up. I was sure I would lose my balance and fall. "No, I'm OK," I answered. I stepped down and immediately I knew something was wrong and that's when the dreaming began.

Another couple had come to the waterfall just before I fell and the husband went to find help. My aunt and the lady had somehow managed to climb down to where I was. I have no idea how long it was before I regained consciousness. When my aunt told me I had fallen I couldn't believe it was happening. I kept my eyes closed most of the time trying not to panic. If I had realized that I had fallen twenty-five feet through the air I would probably have had a heart attack! "Can you wiggle your toes?" they asked. I wiggled them and then asked if my skirt was up because I could feel the air. Without thinking I lifted myself up so they could pull it down. That sudden movement caused me to throw up everything I had eaten for breakfast but it must have comforted my aunt who told me later that she was sure I had broken my neck when I hit the ground. My Aunt and the other lady said they thought my wrist was broken and I opened my eyes long enough to look at it. I had never had a broken bone before so I didn't know what to expect. It was swollen and burning. But by that time I was *upset*! I had just had my hair highlighted and there I was laying with my head in the dirt. That really made me mad! Even more infuriating was the fact that I had managed to get my bills paid up and was even a bit ahead of the financial game and now I was going to have to miss work because of a broken wrist. It's amazing what you worry about before you realize that you could have been killed!

It took the rescue team about two hours to get down to

where we were and for the biggest part of that time I was unconscious. The next thing I remember was hearing men grunt as they carried the gurney I was on up the hill. Then I felt myself slide. My eyes flew open and I said, "I'm falling." A beautiful pair of blue eyes looked into mine and a reassuring voice said, "We've got you." I had just taken a bad fall but I could still appreciate a good looking man! What an inopportune time to pass out again! I did wake up long enough to hear someone saying that a helicopter was coming for me. I had never been on a plane before and I let them know I didn't want to go on one now. A little while later I awoke to feel myself being loaded onto what I thought was an ambulance, I assumed they had listened to me. But I was flying! I don't know how many times I woke up and slipped back into unconsciousness. One man on the helicopter kept yelling at me to wake up and talk to him. He was annoying me because I wanted to sleep. I do believe I managed to tell him that God would take care of me and not to worry before I went to sleep again. I was taken to a hospital in West Virginia and then on to a trauma center in Roanoke, Virginia. My aunt had driven my car back to her house so she could get in touch with my parents so I was alone. Test after test was taken, some while I was conscious and others while I wasn't. A doctor came in to set the bone on side of my left hand which had a clean break. He told me I would have to get a surgeon when I got home because my wrist was pretty messed up. I prayed and really believed that God would heal me so I wouldn't have to go through that. They didn't get done with the last test until late that night and when it came back OK, they were ready to discharge me. God is a Wonder! I fell twenty-five feet through the air and hit the ground *hard* but the hospital didn't even keep me overnight! However my parents still hadn't arrived. It turns out they had gone to Roanoke, West Virginia and had to turn around and come to Roanoke, Virginia. It took them six hours to reach me but by that time I was more alert.

Before leaving an orderly helped me to the restroom and I almost screamed when I looked in the mirror! No one had told me that the left side of my face was badly bruised. I'm still amazed that I didn't lose the sight in my left eye because the area around my eye was a violet purple. My cheekbone was swollen and the muscles near my chin were pushed back under the skin into a large ball. But a tiny scratch at the chin and a minor cut on my hand were the only places that had blood on them. My niece summed up my experience later when she looked at my hands and said, "You went through all of that and only broke one nail!" God is Good!

When I returned to Ohio I went to see a bone specialist and much to my dismay I had to have surgery on my wrist. Pieces of donor bones were put in my wrist and a metal apparatus was attached to the top of my hand. Pins were inserted through that to keep my wrist immobile. That device stayed on for five months and when it came off I had several weeks of therapy. Before the surgery I had a lot of fear. I was anxious about the surgery, scared to death about having that piece of metal inserted in my skin and afraid there would be a lot of pain involved during the recovery period. But God took me through it all with very little pain. As a matter of fact, the only time I had severe pain was the day after the operation. And after getting prayer from one of the ministers at church that pain was gone in less than fifteen minutes. Thank God, I have no memory of the fall. Neither have I ever had a nightmare nor a bad dream about it. Today, other than the scars my wrist is as good as it ever was. God is still a Healer!

It took me a long time to realize that I was a walking miracle. People at church kept saying, Sherry, you are a miracle, few people fall twenty-five feet through the air and live to tell about it. After awhile that made me nervous because I realized that it placed an obligation on me to do more with my life. One day after being called a miracle again, I said, "Lord, I'm not comfortable being a miracle." He replied, "Would you be more comfortable being dead, because that's what you would be if you weren't a miracle." I quickly assured Him that I could handle being a miracle!

I can't tell you how many people told me that I needed to write a book about my tumble from the mountaintop and after some time I felt God wanted me to add my testimony to the book also. Because it's a book about learning lessons and I learned a couple after my fall. The first lesson was learned early on in the experience. It was the week of my surgery and I was on my way to Akron, Ohio with my mother and my friend. I was sitting in the back seat feeling really, really sorry for myself. I kept thinking of all I had to go through yet, surgery, another surgery to remove the device that held my bones secure while they healed and then therapy. Then I started thinking how weird it was that the fall hadn't hurt that much, (of course I was unconscious most of the time), but everything I would have to go through to be healed would be very painful. God spoke to my spirit and said, *"There is a lot more pain involved in the process of healing than there is in the act of being broken.* That's why my people aren't delivered. They would rather stay broken than endure the pain of being healed."

I thought about all of the marriages that have fallen apart. Sometimes, when you've been through so much hurt it seems easier to just let it go as opposed to working through the problems. Because revisiting old wounds can cause severe pain. But I believe that there are times when God ordains a process for us to go through and at the end of the process is our healing. I am a witness that God will take you through!

The second lesson was learned a few months later after the metal apparatus was taken off of my wrist. I had gone to West Virginia and went to visit the Aunt who had been with me during the fall. She asked me if I ever had bad dreams about it and I said I never had. She said, "I couldn't sleep for a long time because every time I closed my eyes I saw you falling. It took me a long time to get over it." Later, the Lord gave me this spiritual revelation of that natural occurrence. When a person backslides and leaves the church and then returns they often get discouraged because folk don't treat them the same as they used to. And sometimes they start feeling like they are not getting the sympathy or encouragement they should receive after coming back to the Lord. But in actuality, the one that left the church is the one that should be *giving* the sympathy and encouragement.

After my accident the Lord healed me and I went on my merry way. I was never traumatized by the fall. *But those around me were.* And for some of them it was a long time before they could close their eyes without repeatedly seeing that fall. The same thing happens in the church. When someone comes back to the Lord and receives forgiveness they bounce back, sometimes on fire for God. They put the past behind them and rush towards the future. But every time they get up to testify someone in the congregation is seeing the fall. Whenever they sing in the choir someone is seeing the fall. And God help them if they should stand at the podium to preach because many will be seeing the fall. It may take some time to erase that picture from their minds because seeing an anointed child of God fall is a traumatic experience. Therefore, *the burden is on the one who fell to be patient and understanding.* Not the other way around

Well, I think the story is over now. I pray that the lessons I learned while having fun and the ones I learned while not having *any* fun will aid you on your journeys through Spiritual valleys, across Spiritual rivers and up Spiritual mountains. Travel well my Friend!

LESSONS LEARNED AS A CHILD
Dedicated to my Mother

I remember growing up in West Virginia and a time when being free, to roam, to play and to explore its scenic beauty meant so much to me. Happiness was running wild from early light until evening's dust began to fall, at the time I didn't know it was God's voice I followed, all I heard was nature's call. For yonder mountains did beckon with dizzying heights that begged to be climbed, while yon stream's hypnotic beat accompanied the wanderlust that sang through my mind. And so, I heeded the call never giving a thought to the worry I caused you way back then, as I began to conquer obstacles that should have seemed impossible to a child not yet ten. Now I'm older and realize that out of fear by your side you could have made me stay, instead out of LOVE and God-given wisdom you let me have my way. By doing so God was able to teach me from nature, spiritual laws I would need to know, lessons I was able to learn as a young child because you loved me enough to let me go.

You let me go, I learned to climb, now there are no mountains that can stand in my way, no spiritual test is unconquerable since I have learned to take time in the valley to pray. I've learned that the valley, that "hated" place, is really a place full of potential power, it is there that God meets us to comfort, develop and direct us during our darkest hour. The valley is where you can stand back and get a clear look at the obstacles you face enabling you to plan and chart your course as you climb towards that destined place. But which mountain to climb first, how to choose when they are everywhere you look, God showed me how to recognize which test I was to prepare for in His Holy Book. David talked about a valley called, The Shadow of Death, his "hated" place had a name, letting him know his valley and the mountain he had to climb were one and the same. His valley was shadowed because Death Mountain stood between David and the sun yet he never mentioned the mountain, the valley was where that battle was really won! You can't prepare to climb up Mount Finance from the Valley of the Shadow of Lust so look for the shadow to guide you, but before you go anywhere, climb Mount Trust. Another lesson that God taught me was to be thankful for the mountain's rough side, in every spiritual test He has given me something to hold on to so that I would not slide. As a child, it was a small tree or even a briar I would grab when I started sliding down, as an adult every victory in God and my failures have gained for me higher ground. A great man once said, *"I have been* to the mountaintop" but he did not remain up there, he had to come down and start over, in mountain climbing that's how you get somewhere. As Saints we hate to Start Over, so we will climb to a certain point and then we stop but it's not possible in the natural or spiritual world to step from mountaintop to mountaintop. Therefore, after we have climbed, reached the top and become victorious over the situation, we must return to our place of power because a Spiritual mountaintop is not designed for habitation.

You let me go, I learned to get over, now there are no rivers I cannot pass through, no spiritual Jordan can defeat me for in early childhood I learned a thing or two. The stream that ran past our old home place was one of my most favorite places to be but because I played there so often the changes being made were ones I could not see. I could step from rock to rock without falling and getting wet, to me it was just a game but God was teaching me how to "Get Over" before I even knew His name. Look before you leap and plan your steps in advance were lessons I leaned well for I became more cautious about the stones I chose to stand on every time I fell! Many times I would jump to a rock thinking that it was solid and firmly set in place only to find out that it was "slippery", I would fall and end up with mud on my face. I know now that only one Rock, Jesus, can hold my weight, He will not let me fall and He is turning my stumbling blocks into stepping stones as I follow His call. I've learned that every decision I make and every step I take has a Divine recompense, I cannot plan for the moment because my steps are guided by thoughts of eternal consequence. Still, the power of pressure is perhaps the most important lesson I will ever learn, it was a revelation from God, a gift from the Holy Spirit that I could never earn. When I went back home after years of being away and looked at the river I used to play in I realized things had changed; the rocks, small and large, were not as they had once been. The current or water pressure had reshaped and displaced those inert pieces of granite, solid rock had been changed by the application of pressure, on and around it. Extreme pressure will shape or destroy, make or break you; its power is at your command, you can flow with the current and be ruined or you can place yourself in the Master's hand. For if water pressure has the power to change the surface of a rock while it lays idle and still, the pressure God allows me to be put under for His glory will mold me into His perfect will.

It's many years later and I'm just now realizing that God was with me all the time, in the Spirit I look back and can feel His presence, can see His hand holding mine. As a child I was taught by the Master Himself how to be a vessel fit for His use, so now, when I am tested in Climbing Higher and Getting Over, I am Without Excuse!

ABOUT THE AUTHOR

Sherry Wyne is the author of five Inspirational books on Amazon.com;

"Lessons Learned In Jumbo Valley"
"A Book About Some Trees - by God"
"God Thoughts in Poetry & Prose"
"From God's Heart To Yours - The Greeting Card Book"
and
"Mother's Day - Greeting Card Book".

Sherry also has a shop, **Sherry Wyne Art** at Redbubble.com where her photo art and designs are featured on products such as clothing, home decor, greeting cards, photo prints and more.

Sherry loves photography and uses her scenic photos on the greeting cards she writes and designs.

Questions or comment please contact sherrywynedesigns@gmail.com

https://www.facebook.com/SherryWyneBooks

SherryWyneArt.redbubble.com

Mom, Me & Nancy

Mom & Dad

Granny & Pappy Green, Pappy & Granny Cutlip
Dad & Mom

Uncle. Dad, Pappy Green, Me, Granny Green, Punk

Mom, Dad
Sissy, Bud, Me & Punk

Dad, Punk, Mom & Sisssy
Bud, Me

Me

Me, Bud, Sissy & Punk

Punk, Me, Bud, Pappy Red

Granny Cutlip, Me, Mom

Dad & Me

Sissy

Bud, Sissy & Punk

Punk, Bud, Me & Sissy

Bud
Sissy
Me
&
Punk

Dad, Sissy, Bud
Mom, Punk, Me

Dad & Mom

The Old Homestead

Our sawdust pile where we played at the top right and Sissy

Home Sweet Home

107

Made in the USA
Middletown, DE
11 July 2022